JEWELS FROM THE WORD & MANNA FOR THE SOUL

Published by God's Love Revealed.
Austin, Texas

ISBN: 978-0-615-26063-1
1. Religion / Christian Ministry / General
2. Religion / Christian Life / Inspirational

JEWELS FROM THE WORD & MANNA FOR THE SOUL

"For God so loved the world that He gave His One and Only Son, that whoever believes in Him shall not perish but have eternal life. For God did not send His Son into the world to condemn the world but to save the world through Him. Whoever believes in Him is not condemned, but whoever does not believe stands condemned already because He has not believed in the name of God's One and Only Son." ***(John 3:16-18)***

CONTENTS

PROLOGUE

These Scriptures are meant to bring you the same hope, encouragement and strength that they have brought me. As a Christian you will go through many trials as you grow and mature in your Christian walk. These trials are to help strengthen your faith and produce Christ like character and perseverance.

(Romans 5:2-5) "And we rejoice in the hope of the glory of God. Not only so, but we also rejoice in our sufferings, because we know that suffering produces perseverance; perseverance, character and character, hope. And hope does not disappoint us, because God has poured out His love into our hearts by the Holy Spirit, whom He has given us."

They are also to sanctify you.

(I Peter 1: 6-9) "In this you greatly rejoice, though now for a little while you may have had to suffer grief in all kinds of trials. These have come so that your faith--of greater worth than gold, which perishes even though refined by fire--may be proved genuine and may result in praise, glory and honor when Jesus Christ is revealed. Though you have not seen Him, you love Him; and even though you do not see Him now, you believe in Him and are filled with an inexpressible and glorious joy, for you are receiving the goal of your faith, the salvation of your souls."

At conversion your heart is changed and you are given a new heart; one that is devoted to God. This does not mean that you are now the perfect Christian. You have lived in the world and according to the world for many years before receiving Jesus Christ into your heart. It will take time for God to renew your mind and clean it up; sanctify it.

(John 17:17) "Sanctify them by the truth; your Word is truth." This is done through trials and reading the Word of God. **(Romans 12:2)**

“Do not conform any longer to the pattern of this world, but be transformed by the renewing of your mind.”

Whatever you put into your mind on a daily basis is what comes out. If you constantly are watching T.V. programs with sex, violence, bad language and completely ungodly ways; these are the things that will fill your mind and heart and “out of the overflow of the heart the mouth speaks”. The people around you influence you as well.

(I Corinthians 15:33) “Do not be mislead; Bad company corrupts good character.”

In all of this, God has not left us helpless. He left us His Word and the Holy Spirit to guide us and help us through life.

(John 16:13) “But when he, the Spirit of Truth comes, he will guide you into all truth. he will not speak on his own; he will speak only what he hears, and He will tell you what is yet to come.”
(Joshua 1:8) “Do not let the Book of the Law depart from your mouth; meditate on it day and night, so that you may be careful to do everything written in it. Then you will be prosperous and successful.”

In the following pages are some Scriptures that are promises from God. If you read these and meditate on them they will be with you in your time of need. God will bring them to your remembrance.

(John 14:26) “But the Counselor, the Holy Spirit, whom the Father will send in My name, will teach you all things and will remind you of everything I have said to you.” In order for God to remind you of what He has said to you, His Word, you must read it.

He cannot remind of something that you have never seen or read. And God exalts his Word; what is in His Word is his will, so pray his Word and reap the harvest from it.

(Psalm 138:2) “For you have exalted above all things your name and your Word.”

God's Word is the strength to get you through your trials no matter how rough they may be. Nothing is too hard for God.

(**Jeremiah 32:27)** "I am the Lord, the God of all mankind. Is anything too hard for Me?"

With Jesus Christ dwelling within you, there is nothing that you can't do or get through.

(Philippians 4:13) "I can do everything through Him who gives me strength."

Chapter 1: God's Faithfulness & His Unconditional Love & Forgiveness

God is faithful and He loves you. He loves you with an *Agape love.* This is an unconditional love, one that loves from the inside out. He sees your heart, that part of you that is hidden from everyone else. He sees all you have done and will do and loves you not because of your actions, but in spite of them. He proved this in Jesus Christ.

(Romans 5:8) "But God demonstrates His own love for us in this: While we were sinners, Christ died for us."

(I John 3:1) "How great is the love the Father has lavished on us, that we should be called children of God!"

His arms are always open to catch you and to forgive you when you fall. He knows we are human and are not perfect and that as hard as we may try, at times we will fall.

(Exodus 15:13) "In Your unfailing love You will lead the people You have redeemed. In Your strength You will guide them to Your holy dwelling."
(Deuteronomy 4:29-31) "But if from there you seek the Lord your God, you will find Him if you look for Him with all your heart and with all your soul. When you are in distress and all these things have happened to you, then in later days you will return to the Lord your God and obey Him. For the Lord your God is a merciful God; He will not abandon or destroy you or forget the covenant with your forefathers, which He confirmed to them by oath."
(Psalm 9:10) "Those who know your name will trust in You, for You, Lord, have never forsaken those who seek You."
(Psalm 18:32) "It is God who arms me with strength and makes my way perfect."
(Psalm 36:5) "Your love, O Lord, reaches to the heavens, your faithfulness to the skies."
(Psalm 103:8-10) "The Lord is compassionate and gracious; slow to anger, abounding in love. He will not always accuse, nor will He

harbor His anger forever; He does not treat us as our sins deserve or repay us according to our iniquities."
(Psalm 103:13) "As a father has compassion on his children, so the Lord has compassion on those who fear Him."
(Psalm 117:1-2) "Praise the Lord, all you nations; extol Him, all you peoples. For great is His love toward us, and the faithfulness of the Lord endures forever."
(Psalm 119:105) "Your Word is a lamp to my feet and a light for my path."
(Psalm 145:13) "The Lord is faithful to all His promises and loving toward all He has made."
(Proverbs 3:5-6) "Trust in the Lord with all your heart and lean not on your own understanding; in all your ways acknowledge Him, and He will make your paths straight."
(Proverbs 23:17-18) "Do not let your heart envy sinners, but always be zealous for the Lord. There is surely a future hope for you and your hope will not be cut off."
(Isaiah 49:23) Those who hope in Me will not be disappointed."
(Isaiah 58:11) "The Lord will guide you always; He will satisfy your needs in a sunscorched land and will strengthen your frame."
(Lamentations 3:22-23) "Because of the Lord's great love we are not consumed, for His compassions never fail. They are new every morning; great is your faithfulness."
(Jeremiah 31:3) "I have loved you with an everlasting love; I have drawn you with loving-kindness."
(I Chronicles 28:20) "Be strong and courageous, and do the work. Do not be afraid or discouraged, for the Lord God, my God, is with you. He will not fail or forsake you until all the work for the service of the temple of the Lord is finished."
(Romans 3:3-4) "What if some did not have faith? Will their lack of faith nullify God's faithfulness? Not at all!"
(Romans 3:23) "For all have sinned and fall short of the glory of God, and are justified freely by His grace through the redemption that came by Christ Jesus."
(I Corinthians 10:12-13) "So, if you think you are standing firm, be careful that you don't fall! No temptation has seized you except what is common to man. And God is faithful; He will not let you be tempted beyond what you can bear. But when you are tempted, He will also provide a way out so that you can stand up under it."

(Romans 8:1) "Therefore, there is now no condemnation for those who are in Christ Jesus, because through Christ Jesus the law of the Spirit of life set me free from the law of sin and death."
(Romans 10:11) "Anyone who trusts in Him will never be put to shame."
(I Corinthians 1:8-9) "He will keep you strong to the end, so that you will be blameless on the day of our Lord Jesus Christ. God, who has called you into fellowship with His Son Jesus Christ our Lord, is faithful."
(I Corinthians 13:8) "Love never fails."
(Galatians 5:22-23) "But the fruit of the Spirit is love, joy, peace, patience, kindness, goodness, faithfulness, gentleness and self-control. Against such things there is no law." (If you are walking in the fruit of the Spirit-no one can take the joy and peace of God away from you.)
(II Timothy 2:13) "If we are faithless, He will remain faithful, for He cannot disown Himself."
(Hebrews 8:12) "For I will forgive their wickedness and will remember their sins no more."
(I John 1:9) "If we confess our sins, He is faithful and just and will forgive us our sins and purify us from all unrighteousness."

Chapter 2: Omnipresence of God & assurance that you are His

God is always with you and nothing can take you away from Him. Even when you blow it from time to time, He is still with you. Once you become His child you **ARE** His. Nothing can separate you from His love or take you from Him. He is a God that loved you so much; He sent His One and Only Son to die in place of you! That alone should tell you just how much God loves you!

(Deuteronomy 31:6) "Be strong and courageous. Do not be afraid or terrified because of them, for the Lord your God goes with you; He will **never** leave you nor forsake you."
(Psalm 23:4) "Even though I walk through the valley of the shadow of death, I will fear no evil, for You are with me."
(Psalm 118:6-7) "The Lord is with me; I will not be afraid. What can man do to me? The Lord is with me; He is my helper. I will look in triumph on my enemies."
(Isaiah 43:1-3) "Fear not, For I have redeemed you; I have summoned you by name; **you are mine**. When you pass through the waters, I will be with you; and when you pass through the rivers, they will not sweep over you. When you walk through the fire, you will not be burned; the flames will not set you ablaze. For I am the Lord, your God, the Holy One of Israel, your Savior."

The trials you go through are to mold you and help you grow as a Christian, but your Heavenly Father will always protect you.

(Isaiah 43:5) "Do not be afraid, for I am with you."
(John 10:27-30) "My sheep listen to My voice; I know them, and they follow Me. I give them eternal life, and they shall never perish; **no one can snatch them out of My hand.** My Father, who has given them to Me, is greater than all; no one can snatch them out of My Father's hand. I and the Father are One."

HOW AWESOME!! PRAISE GOD!!

(John 14:15-17) “If you love Me, you will obey what I command. And I will ask the Father, and He will give you another Counselor to be with you forever--the Spirit of truth. The world cannot accept Him, because it neither sees Him nor knows Him, for He lives with you and will be in you.”
(I Corinthians 6:19-20) “Do you not know that your body is a temple of the Holy Spirit, who is in you, whom you have received from God? You are not your own; you were bought at a price. Therefore honor God with your body.”
(II Corinthians 1:21-22) “Now it is God who makes both us and you stand firm in Christ. He anointed us, set His seal of ownership on us, and put His Spirit in our hearts as a deposit, guaranteeing what is to come.”
(Romans 8:35-39) “Who shall separate us from the love of Christ? Shall trouble or hardship or persecution or famine or nakedness or danger or sword? As it is written: ‘For your sake we face death all day long; we are considered a sheep to be slaughtered.’ No, in all these things we are more than conquerors through Him who loved us. For I am convinced that neither death nor life, neither angels nor demons, neither the present nor the future, nor any powers, neither height nor depth, nor anything else in all creation will be able to separate us from the love of God that is in Christ Jesus our Lord.”
(Ephesians 1:4-6) “For He chose us in Him before the creation of the world to be holy and blameless in His sight. In love He predestined us to be adopted as His sons through Jesus Christ, in accordance with His pleasure and will-- to the praise of His glorious grace, which He has freely given us in the One He loves.”
(Ephesians 1:13-14) “Having believed, you were marked in Him with a seal, the promised Holy Spirit, who is a deposit guaranteeing our inheritance until the redemption of those who are God’s possession--to the praise of His glory.”
(Ephesians 4:30) “And do not grieve the Holy Spirit of God, with whom you were sealed for the day of redemption.”
(James 4:7-8) “Submit yourselves, then, to God. Resist the devil, and he will flee from you. Come near to God and He will come near to you.”
(Philippians 1:6) “Being confident of this, that He who began a good work in you will carry it on to completion until the day of Christ Jesus.”

Chapter 3: God's Ever-Sustaining Love

Your heavenly Father loves you so much that He has stored up for you everything you need. He knows your needs even before you know them yourself.

(Matthew 6:8) "Your Father knows what you need before you ask Him."

But you must ask, you must seek His presence and His will. He will not force Himself on you. He wants you to come to Him out of your own free will and devotion.

(James 4:2) "You do not have, because you do not ask God."

God knows the trials you have to go through are difficult and heartbreaking at times and He has provision for you; but you must ask Him. Just like with your own children; some things in their life they need to learn on their own. You cannot do everything for them. They must learn from trial and error, from their mistakes. Another part of God's love is the free will He gave to all mankind. He wants a love that is given to Him freely, not forced like robots. Free will works both ways. He can whisper into someone's heart to do something that will protect them or someone else, but it is their choice to obey. Just as it is with your own children; you can them tell what to do, and stubbornness with still rear its ugly head from time to time. But you are always there to love, comfort and pick them back up when they need it. So it is with your heavenly Father.

(II Samuel 22:33) "It is God who arms me with strength and makes my way perfect."
(Psalm 18:16-29) "He reached down from on high and took hold of me; He drew me out of deep waters. He rescued me from my powerful enemy, from my foes, who were too strong for me. They confronted me in the day of my disaster, but the Lord was my support. He brought me out into a spacious place; he rescued me because He

delighted in me. The Lord has dealt with me according to my righteousness; according to the cleanness of my hands He has rewarded me. For I have kept the ways of the Lord; I have not done evil by turning from my God. All His laws are before me; I have not turned away from His decrees. I have been blameless before Him and have kept myself from sin. The Lord has rewarded me according to my righteousness, according to the cleanness of my hands in His sight. To the faithful You show Yourself faithful, to the blameless You show Yourself blameless, to the pure You show Yourself pure, but to the crooked You show Yourself shrewd. You save the humble but bring low those who eyes are haughty. You, O Lord, keep my lamp burning; my God turns my darkness into light. With your help I can advance against a troop; with my God I can
scale a wall."

(Psalm 20:4) "May He give you the desire of your heart and make all your plans succeed."

(Psalm 25:3) "No one whose hope is in You will ever be put to shame, but they will be put to shame who are treacherous without excuse."

(Psalm 27:14) "Wait for the Lord; be strong and take heart and wait for the Lord."

(Psalm 28:7) "The Lord is my strength and my shield; my heart trusts in Him and I am helped."

(Psalm 29:11) "The Lord gives strength to His people; the Lord blesses His people with peace."

(Psalm 31:19) How great is Your goodness, which You have stored up for those who fear You, which You bestow in the sight of men on those who take refuge in You."

(Psalm 32:7) "You are my hiding place; You will protect me from trouble and surround me with songs of deliverance."

(Psalm 33:11) "But the plans of the Lord stand firm forever, the purposes of His heart through all generations."

(Psalm 34:17-20) "The righteous cry out, and the Lord hears them; He delivers them from all their troubles. The Lord is close to the brokenhearted and saves those who are crushed in spirit. A righteous man may have many troubles, but the Lord delivers him from them all; He protects all his bones, not one of them will be broken."

(Psalm 37:4) "Delight yourself in the Lord and He will give you the desires of your heart."

(Psalm 46:1) "God is our refuge and strength and ever-present help in times of trouble."
(Psalm 46:10) "Be still, and know that I am God." -- When you don't know what to do and are troubled in a bad situation, take it to God in prayer. Then be still, wait on Him to take care of it. Remember, He is God!!
(Psalm 54:2) "Surely God is my help; the Lord is the one who sustains me."
(Psalm 55:22) "Cast your cares on the Lord and He will sustain you; He will never let the righteous fall."
(Psalm 56:3-4) "When I am afraid, I will trust in You. In God, whose Word I praise, in God I trust; I will not be afraid. What can mortal man do to me?"
(Psalm 73:26) "My flesh and my heart may fail, but God is the strength of my heart and my portion forever."
(Psalm 97:10-11) "Let those who love the Lord hate evil, for He guards the lives of His faithful ones and delivers them from the hand of the wicked. Light is shed upon the righteous and joy on the upright in heart."
(Psalm 103:17) "But from everlasting to everlasting the Lord's love is with those who fear Him, and His righteousness with their children's children."
(Psalm 147:3) "He heals the brokenhearted and binds up their wounds."
(Proverbs 29:25) "Fear of man will prove to be a snare, but whoever trusts in the Lord is kept safe."
(**Psalm 121:7-8)** "The Lord will keep you from all harm—He will watch over your life; the Lord will watch over your coming and going both now and forevermore."
(Psalm 125:1-2) "Those who trust in the Lord are like Mount Zion, which cannot be shaken but endures forever. As the mountains surround Jerusalem, so the Lord surrounds His people both now and forevermore."
(Isaiah 26:3) "You will keep in perfect peace him whose mind is steadfast, because he trusts in You."
(Isaiah 40:28-31) "Do you not know? Have you not heard? The Lord is the everlasting God, the Creator of the ends of the earth. He will not grow tired or weary, and His understanding no one can fathom. He gives strength to the weary and increases the power of the weak. Even

youths grow tired and weary and young men stumble and fall; but those who hope in the Lord will renew their strength. They will soar on wings like eagles; they will run and not grow weary, they will walk and not grow faint."
(Isaiah 41:10) "So do not fear, for I am with you; do not be dismayed, for I am your God. I will strengthen you and help you; I will uphold you with My righteous right hand."
(Isaiah 49:23) "Then you will know that I am the Lord; those who hope in Me will not be disappointed."
(Matthew 19:26) "With man this is impossible, but with God all things are possible."
(I Corinthians 1:8-9) "He will keep you strong to the end, so that you will be blameless on the day of our Lord Jesus Christ. God, who has called you into fellowship with his Son Jesus Christ our Lord, is faithful."
(Ephesians 3:17-18) "And I pray that you, being rooted and established in love, may have power, together with all the saints, to grasp how wide and long and high and deep is the love of Christ, and to know this love that surpasses knowledge--that you may be filled to the measure of all the fullness of God."
(Philippians 4:13) "I can do everything through Him who gives me strength."
(II Thessalonians 3:3) "But the Lord is faithful, and He will strengthen and protect you from the evil on."

Chapter 4: Promises for Lost Loved Ones

Just as Jesus wanted the ones who are His with Him in heaven; He knows how much we love our own family members and He has promises in His Word for you to stand on and pray over for the loved ones in your life who are not saved yet.

(John 17:24) "Father, I want those You have given Me to be with Me where I am, and to see My glory, the glory You have given Me because You loved Me before the creation of the world."
(Deuteronomy 30:6) "The Lord your God will circumcise your hearts and the hearts of your descendants, so that you may love Him with all your heart and with all your soul, and live."
(Psalm 112:1-2) "Praise the Lord. Blessed is the man who fears the Lord, who finds great delight in His commands. His children will be mighty in the land; the generation of the upright will be blessed."
(**Proverbs 11:21**) "Though hand joined in hand, the wicked shall not be unpunished: but the seed of the righteous shall be delivered."
(Proverbs 20:24) "A man's steps are directed by the Lord. How then can anyone understand his own way."
(Proverbs 22:6) "Train a child in the way he should go, and when he is old he will not turn from it."
(Ecclesiastes 3:1) "There is a time for everything, and a season for every activity under heaven."
(Ecclesiastes 8:6) "For there is a proper time and procedure for every matter, though a man's misery weighs heavily upon him."
(Isaiah 42:7-8) "To open the eyes that are blind, to free captives from prison and to release from the dungeon those who sit in darkness. I am the Lord; that is My name!"
(Isaiah 42:16) "I will lead the blind by ways they have not known, along unfamiliar paths I will guide them; I will turn the darkness into light before them and make the rough places smooth. These are the things I will do; I will not forsake them."
(Isaiah 49:8-18) "This is what the Lord says: "In the time of My favor I will answer you, and in the day of salvation I will help you; I will keep you and will make you to be a covenant for the people, to

restore the land and to reassign its desolate inheritances, to say to the captives, 'Come out,' and to those in darkness, 'Be free!'
"They will feed beside the roads and find pasture on every barren hill. They will neither hunger nor thirst, nor will the desert heat or the sun beat upon them. He who has compassion on them will guide them and lead them beside springs of water. I will turn all my mountains into roads, and My highways will be raised up. See, they will come from afar—some from the north, some from the west, some from the region of Aswan." Shout for joy, O heavens; rejoice O earth; burst into song, O mountains! For the Lord comforts His people and will have compassion on His afflicted ones. But Zion said, "The Lord has forsaken me, the Lord has forgotten me." "Can a mother forget the baby at her breast and have no compassion on the child she has borne? Though she may forget, I will not forget you! See, I have engraved you on the palms of My hands; your walls are ever before Me. Your sons hasten back, and those who laid you waste depart from you. Lift up your eyes and look around; all your sons gather and come to you. As surely as I live," declares the Lord, "you will wear them all as ornaments; you will put them on, like a bride."
(Isaiah 49:25) "I will contend with those who contend with you, and your children I will save."
(Isaiah 54:13) "All your son's will be taught by the Lord, and great will be your children's peace."
(Isaiah 55:8-9) "For My thoughts are not your thoughts, neither are your ways My ways,' declares the Lord. 'As the heavens are higher than the earth, so are My ways higher than your ways and My thoughts than your thoughts." --He is God and He knows the beginning and the end of your trial, so things must be done in His way and in His time. If He can create the world and everything in it, He can save your lost loved ones as well.
(Jeremiah 24:7) "I will give them a heart to know Me, that I am the Lord. They will be My people, and I will be their God, for they will return to Me with all their heart."
(Jeremiah 31:16-17) "This is what the Lord says: "Restrain your voice from weeping and your eyes from tears, for your work will be rewarded," declares the Lord. "They will return from the land of the enemy. So there is hope for your future," declares the Lord. "Your children will return to their own land."

(Ezekiel 11:18-21) "They will return to it and remove all its vile images and detestable idols. I will give them an undivided heart and put a new spirit in them; I will remove from them their heart of stone and give them a heart of flesh. Then they will follow My decrees and be careful to My laws. They will be My people, and I will be their God. But as for those whose hearts are devoted to their vile images and detestable idols, I will bring down on their own heads what they have done, declares the Sovereign Lord."

(Matthew 15:28) "Woman, you have great faith! Your request is granted."

(Luke 18:4) "Even though I don't fear God or care about men, yet because this widow keeps bothering me, I will see that she gets justice, so that she won't eventually wear me out with her coming!"

(Luke 18:7-8) "Listen to what the unjust judge says. And will not God bring about justice for His chosen ones, who cry out to Him day and night? Will He keep putting them off? I tell you, He will see that they get justice, and quickly."

(John 1:12-13) "Yet to all who received Him, to those who believed in His name, He gave the right to become children of God--children born not of natural descent, nor of human decision or a husband's will, but born of God."

(John 14:12-14) "I tell you the truth, anyone who has faith in Me will do what I have been doing. He will do even greater things than these, because I am going to the Father. And I will do whatever you ask in My name, so that the Son may bring glory to the Father. You may ask Me for anything in My name, and I will do it."

(Acts 2:38-39) "Repent and be baptized, every one of you, in the name of Jesus Christ for the forgiveness of your sins. And you will receive the gift of the Holy Spirit. This promise is for you and your children and for all who are far off--for all whom the Lord or God will call."

(Acts 11:14) "He will bring you a message through which you and all your household will be saved."

(Acts 16:31) "Believe in the Lord Jesus, and you will be saved--you and your household."

(Romans 4:17) "He is our father in the sight of God, in whom he believed--the God who gives life to the dead and calls things that are not as though they were."

(Romans 4:18) “Against all hope, Abraham in hope, believed and so became the father of many nations.”
(II Corinthians 4:18) “So we fix our eyes not on what is seen, but on what is unseen. For what is seen is temporary, but what is unseen is eternal.”
(Hebrews 11:1) “Faith is being sure of what we hope for and certain of what we do not see.”
(I Thessalonians 5:9-10) “For God did not appoint us to suffer wrath but to receive salvation through our Lord Jesus Christ. He died for us so that, whether we are awake or asleep, we may live together with Him.”
(I Timothy 2:3-4) “This is good and pleases God our Savior, who wants all men to be saved and to come to a knowledge of the truth.”
(II Peter 3:9) “The Lord is not slow in keeping His promise, as some understand slowness. He is patient with you, not wanting anyone to perish, but everyone to come to repentance.”
(I John 5:14) “This is the confidence we have in approaching God: that if we ask anything according to His will, He hears us. And if we know that He hears us--whatever we ask—we know that we have what we asked of Him.”

Chapter 5: Promises for Victory & Deliverance

The battle belongs to God and victory is promised to you with all thanks and praise to our Lord and Savior Jesus Christ. Satan is trying to destroy God's children. His time is short and he is trying to take as many people with him as he can.

(John 10:10) "The thief comes to steal, and kill and destroy; I have come that they may have life, and have it to the full."

Satan destroys your soul, and he is the one who makes you feel dead inside, Jesus gives life.

(Ephesians 4:14) "Wake up, O sleeper, and rise from the dead, and Christ will shine on you."

Put your love, trust and faith in God and worship and obey Him and victory in your trials will be yours as well as victory over them.

(Deuteronomy 7:22) "The Lord your God will drive out those nations before you, little by little. You will not be allowed to eliminate them all at once, or the wild animals will multiply around you."
(Deuteronomy 11:22-23) "If you carefully observe all these commands I am giving you to follow--to love the Lord your God, to walk in all His ways and to hold fast to Him--then the Lord will drive out all these nations before you, and you will dispossess nations larger and stronger than you."
(Deuteronomy 20:3-4) "Hear, O Israel, today you are going into battle against your enemies. Do not be fainthearted or afraid; do not be terrified or give way to panic before them. For the Lord your God is the One who goes with you to fight for you against your enemies to give you victory."
(Deuteronomy 31:8) "The Lord Himself goes before you and will be with you; He will never leave you nor forsake you. Do not be afraid;

do not be discouraged."-- He goes before you through your trials, so trust Him. -- He has already been through your trial ahead of you and knows what to do and what to give you to lead you into victory!
(Job 11:7-9) "Can you fathom the mysteries of God? Can you probe the limits of the Almighty? They are higher than the heavens--what can you do? They are deeper than the depths of the grave--what can you know? Their measure is longer than the earth and wider than the sea."
(Psalm 3:8) "From the Lord comes deliverance. May your blessing be on your people."
(**Psalm 18:16-19**) "He reached down from on high and took hold of me; He drew me out of deep waters. He rescued me from my powerful enemy, from my foes, who were too strong for me. They confronted me in the day of my disaster, but the Lord was my support. He brought me out into a spacious place; He rescued me because He delighted in me."
(Psalm 18:35) "You give me Your shield of victory, and Your right hand sustains me."
(Psalm 44:3) "It was not by their sword that they won the land, nor did their arm bring them victory; it was Your right hand, Your arm, and the light of Your face, for You loved them."
(Psalm 44:6-8) "I do not trust in my bow, my sword does not bring me victory; but You give us victory over our enemies, You put our adversaries to shame. In God we make our boast all day long, and we will praise Your name forever."
(Psalm 50:14-15) "Sacrifice thank offerings to God, fulfill your vows to the Most High, and call upon Me in the day of trouble; I will deliver you and you will honor Me."
(Psalm 60:12) "With God we will gain the victory, and He will trample down our enemies."
(Psalm 72:4) "He will defend the afflicted among the people and save the children of the needy; He will crush the oppressor."
(Psalm 81:13-14) "If My people would but listen to me, if Israel would follow my ways, how quickly would I subdue their enemies and turn My hand against their foes."
(Psalm 118:14-15) "The Lord is my strength and my song; He has become my salvation. Shouts of joy and victory resound in the tents of the righteous: The Lord's right hand has done mighty things!"

(Psalm 119:9-11) "How can a young man keep his way pure? By living according to your Word. I seek You with all my heart; do not let me stray from Your commands. I have hidden Your Word in my heart that I might not sin against You." **--This brings you victory!**
(Proverbs 16:9) "In his heart a man plans his course, but the Lord determines his steps."
(Proverbs 19:21) "Many are the plans in a man's heart, but it is the Lord's purpose that prevails."
(Proverbs 21:30-31) "There is no wisdom, no insight, no plan that can succeed against the Lord. The horse is made ready for the day of battle, but victory rests with the Lord."
(Isaiah 35:4) "Be strong, do not fear; your God will come, He will come with vengeance; with divine retribution He will come to save you."
(Isaiah 43:13) "No one can deliver out of My hand. When I act, who can reverse it?"
(Isaiah 51:5) "My righteousness draws near speedily, My salvation is on the way, and My arm will bring justice to the nations."
(Isaiah 54:17) "No weapon formed against you will prevail, and you will refute every tongue that accuses you."
(Jeremiah 29:11-14) "I know the plans I have for you, declares the Lord, plans to prosper you and not to harm you, plans to give you hope and a future. Then you will call upon Me and come and pray to Me, and I will listen to you. You will seek Me and find Me when you seek Me with all your heart. I will be found by you, declares the Lord, and bring you back from captivity."
(Jeremiah 30:17) "But I will restore you to health and heal your wounds, declares the Lord."
(Jeremiah 31:2) "The people who survive the sword will find favor in the desert; I will come to give rest to Israel."
(II Chronicles 20:15) "Do not be afraid or discouraged because of this vast army. For the battle is not yours, but God's."
(II Chronicles 20:17) "You will not have to fight this battle. Take up your positions; stand firm and see the deliverance the Lord will give you, O Judah and Jerusalem."
(Matthew 6:33) "But seek first the His kingdom and His righteousness, and all these things will be given to you as well."
(Romans 8:31) "What, then, shall we say in response to this? If God is for us, who can be against us?"

(I Corinthians 15:54-58) "Death has been swallowed up in victory. Where, O death, is your victory? Where, O death, is your sting? The sting of death is sin, and the power of sin is the law. But thanks be to God! He gives us the victory through our Lord Jesus Christ. Therefore, my brothers, stand firm. Let nothing move you. Always give yourselves fully to the work of the Lord, because you know that your labor in the Lord is not in vain."
(I John 5:3-6) "This is love for God: to obey His commands. And His commands are not burdensome, for everyone born of God overcomes the world. This is the victory that overcomes the world, even our faith. Who is it that overcomes the world? Only he who believes that Jesus is the Son of God. This is the one who came by water and blood—Jesus Christ."

Psalm 91 is a beautiful Psalm that tells of God's deliverance, healing, protection and salvation and His ever watchful eye on all those that He loves and that love Him. David was a man who was a man after God's heart. He was not perfect, but he was sincere and truthful. He repented and devoted himself to God. God watched over him and protected him. As you love trust and obey Him, He will do the same for you. I can't think of a better way to close this chapter than to end it with Psalm 91. It is a beautiful Scripture and if you let it, it will speak right to your heart.

"He who dwells in the shelter of the Most High will rest in the shadow of the Almighty. I will say of the Lord, 'He is my refuge and my fortress, my God, in whom I trust.' Surely He will save you from the fowler's snare and from the deadly pestilence. He will cover you with His feathers, and under His wings you will find
refuge; His faithfulness will be your shield and rampart. You will not fear the terror of night, nor the arrow that flies by day, nor the pestilence that stalks in the darkness, nor the plague that destroys at midday. A thousand may fall at your side, ten thousand at your right hand, but it will not come near you. You will only observe with your eyes and see the punishment of the wicked. If you make the Most High your dwelling--even the Lord, who is my refuge-then no harm will befall you, no disaster will come near your tent. For He will command His angels concerning you to guard you in all your ways;

they will lift you up in their hands, so that you will not strike your foot against a stone. You will tread upon the lion
and the cobra; you will trample the great lion and the serpent.
'Because he loves Me,' says the Lord, I will rescue him; I will protect him, for he acknowledges My name. He will call upon Me, and I will answer him; I will be with him in trouble, I will deliver him and honor him. With long life will I satisfy him and show him My salvation."

Chapter 6: Promises for Blessings

(Revelation 22:14) "Blessed are those who wash their robes, that they may have the right to the tree of life and may go through the gates into the city."

Blessings from the Lord are a wonderful showing of God's love. Yet nothing can compare to the gift of eternal life. He gave us His One and Only Son to be the atoning sacrifice for our sins! That should be blessing enough for us all, since there is no one here on earth that can live up to the righteousness of God on their own merits. It is when He purifies your heart that you receive the best blessing of all. The peace and assurance in your heart tells you that your sins are forgiven and you have received the gift of His salvation.

(Exodus 3:21-22) "And I will make the Egyptians favorably disposed toward this people, so that when you leave you will not go empty-handed. Every woman is to ask her neighbor and any woman living in her house for articles of silver and gold and for clothing, which you will put on your sons and daughters. And so you will plunder the Egyptians."

(Deuteronomy 6:10-13) "When the Lord your God brings you into the land He swore to your fathers, to Abraham, Isaac and Jacob, to give you—a land with large, flourishing cities you did not build, houses filled with all kinds of good things you did not provide, wells you did not dig, and vineyards and olive groves you did not plant—then when you eat and are satisfied, be careful that you do not forget the Lord, who brought you out of Egypt, out of the land of slavery. Fear the Lord your God, serve Him only and take your oaths in His name."

(Deuteronomy 28:1-8) "If you fully obey the Lord your God and carefully follow all His commands I give you today, the Lord your God will set you high above all the nations on earth. All these blessings will come upon you and accompany you if you obey the Lord your God: You will be blessed in the city and blessed in the country. The fruit of your womb will be blessed, and the crops of your land and the young of your livestock--the calves of your herds and the lambs of your flocks. Your basket and your kneading trough will be blessed. You will be blessed when you come in and blessed when you go out. The Lord will grant that the enemies who rise up against you will be defeated before you. They will come at you from one direction but flee from you in seven. The Lord will send a blessing on your barns and on everything you put your hands to. The Lord your God will bless you in the land He is giving you."

(Deuteronomy 30:2-3) "And when you and your children return to the Lord your God and obey Him with all your heart and with all your soul according to everything I command you today, then the Lord your God will restore your fortunes and have compassion on you and gather you again from all the nations where He scattered you."

(Joshua 1:8) "Do not let the Book of the Law depart from your mouth; meditate on it day and night, so that you may be careful to do everything written in it. Then you will be prosperous and successful."

(Job 8:7) "Your beginnings will seem humble, so prosperous will your future be."

(Psalm 2:12) "Blessed are all who take refuge in Him."

(Psalm 5:12) "For it is You who blesses the righteous man, O Lord, You surround him with favor as with a shield."

(Psalm 31:19) "How great is your goodness, which you have stored up for those who fear you, which you bestow in the sight of men on those who take refuge in you."

(Psalm 34:8-10) "Taste and see that the Lord is good; blessed is the man who takes refuge in Him. Fear the Lord, you His saints, for those who fear him lack nothing. The lions may grow weak and hungry, but those who seek the Lord lack no good thing."

(Psalm 103:2-5) "Praise the Lord, O my soul, and forget not all His benefits--who forgives all your sins and heals all your diseases, who redeems your life from the pit and crowns you with love and compassion, who satisfies your desires with good things so that your youth is renewed like the eagle's."

(Psalm 112:1-9) "Praise the Lord. Blessed is the man who fears the Lord, who finds great delight in His commands. His children will be mighty in the land; the generation of the upright will be blessed.

Wealth and riches are in his house, and his righteousness endures forever. Even in darkness light dawns for the upright, for the gracious and compassionate and righteous man. Good will come to him who is generous and lends freely, who conducts his affairs with justice. Surely he will never be shaken; a righteous man will be remembered forever. He will have no fear of bad news; his heart is steadfast, trusting in the Lord. His heart is secure, he will have no fear; in the end he will look in triumph on his foes. He has scattered abroad his gifts to the poor, his righteousness endures forever; his horn will be lifted high in honor."

(Psalm 119:1-3) "Blessed are they whose ways are blameless, who walk according to the law of the Lord. Blessed are they who keep His statutes and seek Him with all their heart. They do nothing wrong; they walk in His ways."

(Psalm 128:1-4) "Blessed are all who fear the Lord, who walk in His ways. You will eat the fruit of your labor; blessings and prosperity will be yours. Your wife will be like a fruitful vine within your house; your sons will be like olive shoots around your table. Thus is the man blessed who fears the Lord."

(Proverbs 3:33) "The Lord's curse is on the house of the wicked, but He blesses the home of the righteous."

(Proverbs 8:32-36) "Now then, My sons, listen to Me; blessed are those who keep My ways. Listen to My instruction and be wise; do not ignore it. Blessed is the man who listens to Me, watching daily at My doors, waiting at My doorway. For whoever finds Me finds life and receives favor from the Lord. But whoever fails to find Me harms himself; all who hate Me love death."

(Proverbs 10:6-7) "Blessings crown the head of the righteous, but violence overwhelms the mouth of the wicked. The memory of the righteous will be a blessing, but the name of the wicked will rot."

(Proverbs 10:22) "The blessing of the Lord brings wealth, and He adds no trouble to it."

(Malachi 3:8-12) "Will a man rob God? Yet you rob Me. But you ask, 'How do we rob you?' In tithes and offerings. You are under a curse--the whole nation of you--because you are robbing Me. Bring the whole tithe into the storehouse, that there may be food in My house. Test Me in this,' says the Lord Almighty, 'and see if I will not throw open the floodgates of heaven and pour out so much blessing that you will not have room enough for it. I will prevent pests from devouring your crops, and the vines in your fields will not cast their fruit,' says the Lord Almighty. 'Then all the nations will call you blessed, for yours will be a delightful land,' says the Lord Almighty."

(Matthew 5:7) "Blessed are the merciful, for they will be shown mercy."

(John 10:10) "The thief comes to steal, and kill and destroy; I have come that they may have life, and have it to the full."

(Galatians 3:13-14) "Christ redeemed us from the curse of the Law by becoming a curse for us, for it is written, 'Cursed is everyone who is hung on a tree.' He redeemed us in order that the blessing given to Abraham might come to the Gentiles through Christ Jesus, so that by faith we might receive the promise of the Spirit."

(Ephesians 1:3) "Praise be to the God and Father of our Lord Jesus Christ, who has blessed us in the heavenly realms with every spiritual blessing in Christ."

(James 1:12) "Blessed is the man who perseveres under trial, because when he has stood the test, he will receive the crown of life that God has promised to those who love Him."

(II Peter 1:3-4) "His divine power has given us everything we need for life and godliness through our knowledge of Him who called us by His own glory and goodness. Through these He has given us His very great and precious promises, so that through them you may participate in the divine nature and escape the corruption in the world caused by evil desires."

Chapter 7: Scriptures on God's Love

I saved the best chapter for last; scriptures about the love of God. To make it through life and all of its challenges we must be confident in who God is and His love for you. When you are confident in God's love for you and for all of mankind your faith in Him and His promises for you and your life will come easy. Faith is the power of God to help us to stand and to face every trial and every attack of the devil in confidence knowing that no matter what you are facing and no matter what challenges come your way it will always end in victory!

Exodus 15: 13-14 -- "In Your unfailing love You will lead the people You have redeemed. In Your strength You will guide them to Your holy dwelling. The nations will hear and tremble;"
Exodus 34: 6-7 -- "The Lord, the Lord, the compassionate and gracious God, slow to anger, abounding in love and faithfulness, maintaining love to thousands, and forgiving wickedness, rebellion and sin."
Numbers 14:18 -- "The Lord is slow to anger, abounding in love and forgiving sin and rebellion."
Deuteronomy 5:10 -- "but showing love to a thousand generations, of those who love Me and keep My commandments."
Deuteronomy 7:7 -- "The Lord did not set His affections on you and chose you because you were more numerous than other peoples, for you were the fewest of all peoples. But it was because the Lord loved you and kept the oath He swore to your forefathers that He brought you out with a mighty hand and redeemed you from the land of slavery, from the power of Pharaoh King of Egypt."
Deuteronomy 7:9 -- "Know therefore that the Lord your God is God, He is the faithful God, keeping His covenant of love to a thousand generations of those who love Him and keep His commands."
Deuteronomy 7:12-13 --"If you pay attention to these laws and are careful to follow them, then the Lord your God will keep His covenant of love with you as He swore to your forefathers. He will love you and bless you and increase your numbers."

Deuteronomy 10:15 -- "Yet the Lord set His affection on your forefathers and loved them and He chose you, their descendants, above all the nations, as it is today."
Deuteronomy 10:18 -- "He defends the cause of the fatherless and the widow, and loves the alien, giving him food and clothing"
Deuteronomy 23:5 -- "However, the Lord your God would not listen to Balaam but turned the curse into a blessing for you, because the Lord your God loves you."
I Chronicles 16:34 -- "Give thanks to the Lord, for He is good; His love endures forever."
Psalm 25:6 -- "Remember, O Lord, you great mercy and love, for they are from old."
Psalm 25:10 -- "All the ways of the Lord are loving and faithful for those who keep the demands of His covenant."
Psalm 36:5 -- "Your love, O Lord, reaches to the heavens, your faithfulness to the skies."
Psalm 37:28 -- "For the Lord loves the just and will not forsake His faithful ones. They will be protected forever."
Psalm 44:3 -- "It was not by their sword that they won the land, nor did their arm bring them victory; it was your right hand, your arm, and the light of your face, for you loved them."
Psalm 57:10 -- "For great is your love, reaching to the heavens; your faithfulness reaches to the skies."
Psalm 66:20 -- "Praise be to God, who has not rejected my prayer or withheld His love from me!"
Psalm 103:11 -- "For as high as the heavens are above the earth, so great is His love for those who fear Him;"
Psalm 108:6 -- "Save us and help us with your right hand that those you love may be delivered."
Psalm 117:1-2 --" Praise the Lord, all you nations; extol Him, all you peoples. For great is His love toward us, and the faithfulness of the Lord endures forever. Praise the Lord."

Psalm 136 --

"Give thanks to the Lord, for He is good.
His love endures forever.
Give thanks to the God of Gods.
His love endures forever.
Give thanks to the Lord of Lords.
His love endures forever.
to Him who alone does great wonders,
His love endures forever.
who by His understanding made the
heavens, *His love*
endures forever.
who spread out the earth upon the waters.
His love endures forever.
who made the great lights----
His love endures forever.
the sun to govern the day,
His love endures forever.
the moon and stars to govern the night;
His love endures forever.
to Him who struck down the first born of
Egypt
His love endures forever.
and brought Israel out from among them
His love endures forever.
with a mighty hand and outstretched arm;
His love endures forever.
to Him who divided the Red Sea asunder.
His love endures forever.
and brought Israel through the midst of it,
His love endures forever.
but swept Pharaoh and his army into the Red Sea;
His love endures forever.
to Him who led His people through the
desert,
His love endures forever.
who struck down great kings,
His love endures forever.
and killed mighty kings-----

His love endures forever.
Sihon King of the Amorites
His love endures forever.
and Og King of Bashan----
His love endures forever.
and gave their land as an inheritance,
His love endures forever.
an inheritance to His servant Israel;
His love endures forever.
to the one who remembered us in our low
estate
His love endures forever.
and freed us from our enemies,
His love endures forever.
and who gives food to every creature.
His love endures forever.
Give thanks to the God of heaven.
His love endures forever."

Psalm 138:1-3 -- "I will praise You, O Lord, with all my heart; before the "gods" I will sing Your praise. I will bow down toward Your holy temple and will praise Your name for Your love and Your faithfulness, for You have exalted above all things Your name and Your Word. When I called, You answered me; You made me bold and stouthearted."
Psalm 138:6-8 -- "Though the Lord is on high, He looks upon the lowly, but the proud He knows from afar. Though I walk in the midst of trouble, You preserve my life; You stretch out Your hand against the anger of my foes, with Your right hand You save me. The Lord will fulfill His purpose for me; Your love, O Lord, endures forever- do not abandon the works of Your hands."
Psalm 145:13 -- "The Lord is faithful to all His promises and loving toward all He has made."
Proverbs 3:11-12 --" My son, do not despise the Lord's discipline and do not resent His rebuke, because the Lord disciplines those He loves, as a father the son he delights in."
Proverbs 8: 17 -- "I love those who love Me, and those who seek Me find Me."

Proverbs 16:6--"Through love and faithfulness sin is atoned for; through the fear of the Lord a man avoids evil."
Isaiah 54:10 -- "Though the mountains be shaken and the hills be removed, yet My unfailing love for you will not be shaken nor My covenant of peace be removed," says the Lord, who has compassion on you."
Jeremiah 31:3 -- "I have loved you with and everlasting love; I have drawn you with loving kindness."
Lamentations 3:22 --"Because of the Lord's great love we are not consumed, for His compassion never fails."
Lamentations 3: 32-33 --"Though He brings grief, He will show compassion, so great is His unfailing love for He does not willingly bring affliction or grief to the children of men."
Zephaniah 3:17 -- "The Lord your God is with you, He is mighty to save. He will take great delight in you, He will quiet you with His love, He will rejoice over you with singing."
John 3:16 -- "For God so loved the world that He gave His One and Only Son, that whoever believes in Him shall not perish but have eternal life."
John 5:20-21 -- "For the Father loves the Son and shows Him all He does. Yes, to your amazement He will show Him even greater things than these. For just as the Father raises the dead and gives them life, even so the Son gives life to whom He is pleased to give it."
John 14:21 -- "Whoever has My commands and obeys them, He is the one who loves Me. He who loves Me will be loved by My Father, and I too will love him and show Myself to him."
John 15:12-13 -- "Love each other as I have loved you. Greater love has no one than this that he lay down his life for his friends."
Romans 5: 2-5 -- "And we rejoice in the hope of the glory of God not only so, but we also rejoice in our sufferings, because we know that suffering produces perseverance; perseverance, character; and character, hope. And hope does not disappoint us, because God has poured out His love into our hearts by the Holy Spirit, whom He has given us."
Romans 5:8 -- "But God demonstrates His own love for us in this: while we were still sinners, Christ died for us."
Romans 8:37-39 -- "No, in all these things we are more than conquerors through Him who loved us. For I am convinced that

neither death nor life, neither angels nor demons, neither the present nor the future, nor any powers, neither height nor depth, nor anything else in all creation, will be able to separate us from the love of God that is in Christ Jesus our Lord."

I Corinthians 2:9 -- "No eye has seen, no ear has heard, no mind has conceived what God has prepared for those who love Him."

Galatians 2:20 -- "The life I live in the body, I live by faith in the Son of God, who loved me and gave Himself for me."

Ephesians 1:4-6 -- "For He chose us in Him before the creation of the world to be holy and blameless in His sight. In love He predestined us to be adopted as His sons through Jesus Christ, in accordance with His pleasure and will-- to the praise of His glorious grace, which He has freely given us in the One He loves."

Ephesians 2:4 -- "But because of His great love for us, God, who is rich in mercy, made us alive with Christ even when we were dead in transgressions-- it is by grace you have been saved."

Ephesians 3:17-19 -- " And I pray that you, being rooted and established in love, may have power together with all the saints, to grasp how wide and long and high and deep is the love of Christ, and to know this love that surpasses knowledge-- that you be filled to the measure of all the fullness of God."

Ephesians 5:1-2 -- " Be imitators of God, therefore, as dearly loved children and live a life of love, just as Christ loved us and gave Himself up for us as a fragrant offering and sacrifice to God."

II Thessalonians 2:13 -- "But we ought always to thank God for you, brothers loved by the Lord, because from the beginning God chose you to be saved through the sanctifying work of the Spirit and through belief in the truth."

II Thessalonians 2:16 -- "May our Lord Jesus Christ Himself and God our Father, who loved us and by His grace gave us eternal encouragement and good hope, encourage your hearts and strengthen you in every good deed and word."

Hebrews 12: 5-6 -- " My son, do not make light of the Lord's discipline, and do not lose heart when He rebukes you, because the Lord disciplines those He loves, and He punishes everyone He accepts as a son."

James 1: 12 -- "Blessed is the man who perseveres under trial, because when he has stood the test, he will receive the crown of life that God has promised to those who love Him."

I John 3: 1-- "How great is the love the Father has lavished on us that we should be called children of God!"
I John 4: 7-10 -- "Dear friends, let us love one another, for love comes from God. Everyone who loves has been born of God and knows God. Whoever does not love does not know God, because God is love. This is how God showed His love among us: He sent His One and Only Son into the world that we might live through Him. This is love: not that we loved God, but that He loved us and sent His Son as an atoning sacrifice for our sins."
I John 4: 19 -- "We love because He first loved us."
I John 4:15-17 -- "If anyone acknowledges that Jesus is the Son of God, God lives in Him and He in God. And so we know and rely on the love God has for us. God is love. Whoever lives in love lives in God, and God in Him. In this way, love is made complete among us so that we will have confidence on the Day of Judgment, because in the world we are like Him."
II John 1-3 -- "To the chosen lady and her children, whom I love in the truth-- and not I only, but also all who know the truth, which lives in us and will be with us forever: Grace, mercy and peace from God the Father and from Jesus Christ, the Father's Son, will be with us in truth and love."
Jude 1-2 -- "To those who have been called, who are loved by God the Father and kept by Jesus Christ: mercy, peace and love be yours in abundance."
Revelation 3:19 --"Those whom I love I rebuke and discipline. So be earnest and repent."

Epilogue

Your heavenly Father has already placed eternity in your heart. **(Ecclesiastes 3:11)** "He has made everything beautiful in its time. He has also set eternity in the hearts of men; yet they cannot fathom what God has done from beginning to end." If you would draw upon His Holy Word and the Holy Spirit within your heart, He will lead you and guide you and open up the windows of heaven before you. No matter what you go through, the outcome in the hands of Jesus Christ is always victory!

Let the Lord speak to your heart through His Word. As you read His Word and come across Scriptures that have a direct correlation to the trial or situation you are going through, they will jump right out and touch your heart in a special way. You will just know that it is a special Word from God. But in order for God to speak to your heart through His Word you must read it!

As you read the Word of God it will bring comfort to your heart and soul. Your spirit will be renewed and refreshed even in times when you are so down and depressed that you do not feel like doing anything, much less reading. Make yourself! That is when you need it the most!

(Psalm 103:2-5) "Praise the Lord, O my soul, and forget not all His benefits—who forgives all your sins and heals all your diseases, who redeems your life from the pit and crowns you with love and compassion, who satisfies your desires with good things so that your youth is renewed like the eagle's."

Call on your heavenly Father and let Him carry you. Surrender all your worries, all your dreams and your will and let your heavenly Father carry you through to the end of your trial. As you trust in Him and call on His name He will refresh and renew your spirit within you.

(II Corinthians 4:16) "Therefore we do not lose heart. Though outwardly we are wasting away, yet inwardly we are being renewed day by day."

Your heavenly Father loves you so much that He sent His One and Only Son to die for your sins.

(John 3:16-18) "For God so loved the world that He gave His One and Only Son, that whoever believes in Him shall not perish but have eternal life. For God did not send His Son into the world to condemn the world but to save the world through Him. Whoever believes in Him is not condemned, but whoever does not believe stands condemned already because He has not believed in the name of God's One and Only Son."

If God, would send His Son to suffer from humiliation and be beaten beyond human recognition so that we would have life eternally through Him, do you think that after all He went through for us, He would leave us here helpless to fight of Satan and his army of demons by our self? Not at all! He did it so that we would have victory over every area of our lives! Praise God!

(Psalm 107:19-21) "Then they cried to the Lord in their trouble, and He saved them from their distress. He sent forth His Word and healed them; He rescued them from the grave. Let them give thanks to the Lord for His unfailing love and His wonderful deeds for men."

God is truly awesome and if you let Him into your hearts and lives He will guide through to victory in every situation and trial that comes your way.

(John 15:5) "I am the vine; you are the branches. If a man remains in Me and I in him, he will bear much fruit; apart from Me you can do nothing."

God is pure love and all love comes from Him.

(I John 4:16-18) "And so we know and rely on the love God has for us. God is love. Whoever lives in love lives in God, and God in Him.

In this way, love is made complete among us so that we will have confidence on the Day of Judgment, because in this world we are like Him. There is no fear in love. But perfect love drives out fear, because fear has to do with punishment. The one who fears is not made perfect in love."

No one can truly comprehend just how much He loves us and what He has in store for us. Let His love flow through you and you will know peace beyond all understanding.

(Philippians 4: 6-7) "Do not be anxious about anything, but in everything, by prayer and petition, with thanksgiving, present your requests to God. And the peace of God, which transcends all understanding, will guard your hearts and your minds in Christ Jesus."

Just let yourself trust in God. Let His Word guide you and speak to your heart. You will see and know the love and glory of God. He has blessing upon blessing stored up for you. Trust in Him and rest in His presence. Let Him be glorified through you. You will always be a victor! Praise and Glory be to God for His unfailing and never-ending love!

(Psalm 57:5) "Be exalted, O God, above the heavens; let Your glory be over all the earth."

If you are yet saved I invite you to read on through the next few pages and pray the prayer at the end. It will be the best thing you have ever done.

GOD LOVES YOU!

(Jeremiah. 31:3 "I have loved you with an
everlasting love; I have drawn you with loving kindness.")

I Timothy 2:3-4 "God our Savior, who wants all men to be saved and to come to the knowledge of the truth."

He will not knock on the door to your heart forever. Will you let Him in? Ask!

Revelation 3:20 "Here I am! I stand at the door and knock. If anyone hears My voice and opens the door, I will come in and eat with him, and he with Me."

Jesus is the only way to God.

John 14:6 "I am the way, the truth and the life. No one comes to the Father except through Me."
John 3:3 "I tell you the truth, no one can see the kingdom of God unless he is born again."

And, you must make Him Lord of your life.
Matthew 6:24 "No one can serve two masters."
Matthew 7:21 "Not everyone who says to Me, 'Lord, Lord', will enter the kingdom of heaven, but only he who does the will of My Father who is in heaven."

We must leave our old ways behind.

Mark 3:25 "If a house is divided against itself, that house cannot stand."

**You can't live according to the flesh and
desires of the sinful nature and expect to have Jesus in your heart.
He is holy. He is love. Love and Hate cannot exist together.**

Ephesians 4:22-24 "You were taught, with regard to your former way of life, to put off your old self, which is being corrupted by its deceitful desires; to be made new in the attitude of your minds; and to put on the new self, created to be like God in true righteousness and holiness."

God gives you the ability to do His will. He knows it is hard.

Philippians 4:13 "I can do everything through Him who gives me strength."
Romans 3:23 "for all have sinned and fall short of the glory of God."
I John 1:9 "If we confess our sins, He is
faithful and just and will forgive us our sins and purify us from all unrighteousness."
John 1:12 "Yet to all who received Him, to
those who believed in His name, He gave the right to become children of God."
Romans 10:10 "For it is with your heart that you believe and are justified, and it is with your mouth that you confess and are saved."

Then after you confess and ask forgiveness and receive Jesus into your heart, you must testify (tell someone) and be baptized. In this, God is glorified and others might be saved by your example.

II Timothy 1:8 "So do not be ashamed to
testify about our Lord"
I Peter 3:21 "and this water symbolizes baptism that now saves you also-not the removal of dirt from the body but the pledge of a good conscience toward God. It saves you by the resurrection of Jesus

Invitation to Salvation Prayer

Dear Almighty Father in heaven, I know that I am a sinner and I ask your forgiveness of all my sins. I want to make You the Lord of my life and I want to serve You all the days of my life. I believe that Jesus Christ died on the cross for my sins. Thank You so much for loving me and waiting on me to come to the knowledge of the truth! Thank You for my salvation. Please help me and guide me in learning Your Word so I can be a light to the world. Please, Jesus come into my heart, and baptize me with Your Holy Spirit. I thank You and praise Your Holy Name and ask all this in the name of Jesus Christ our Lord. Amen.

www.ingramcontent.com/pod-product-compliance
Lightning Source LLC
LaVergne TN
LVHW050948080826
845145LV00004B/1452

* 9 7 8 0 6 1 5 2 6 0 6 3 1 *